THE BASICS OF
WINNING
ROULETTE

J. Edward Allen

- Gambling Research Institute -
Cardoza Publishing

Fourth Edition

Copyright © 1985, 1993, 1998, 2002 by Cardoza Publishing
- All Rights Reserved -

ISBN: 1-58042-059-1
Library of Congress Catalog No: 2002101903

Table of Contents

Illustrations & Charts

Illustrations

Charts

In the Chips!

I. Introduction

Roulette is a game that has fascinated and intrigued millions of players over the years. It's not only a leisurely game, but an exciting game as well.

You'll be playing the same game that has attracted kings and queens, prime ministers and statesmen, millionaires and captains of industry.

Roulette has a great variety of bets available; more than in any other casino table game. Betting choices may be paid off anywhere from even-money to 35-1, and bets can be made in overlapping fashion with the same numbers covered in several ways.

Because of this factor, the game has attracted systems to beat it from the first time it was introduced. We'll show you the more popular ones and the pitfalls involved.

You'll find out about both the American and European game, including the possible wagers and payoffs involved, so that you'll be able to play this most fascinating of games intelligently.

II. American Roulette

The Dealer

In American casinos, the game is run by one dealer. This is in contrast to the European version of roulette in which several **croupiers** (the French term for dealer) are used, for the European game is played with a double layout, and more employees are needed to staff the table.

But in American casinos, one dealer will suffice to run the game. Sometimes, if the game is particularly busy, the dealer may have an assistant, whose sole function will be to collect losing chips and stack them up. But this is the exception, rather than the rule.

The dealer has several duties. He or she will first change the player's cash into roulette chips. Each player will receive roulette chips of a different color from the other players' chips. These roulette chips have no intrinsic value away from the roulette table and are specially marked. The different colors make for a smoother game, since there will usually be a multitude of bets on the layout, and the only way the dealer will know how to make proper payoffs will be through the color of the chips.

In addition to changing cash for chips, the dealer runs the game. He keeps the wheel in spin, and spins a small white ball counter to the wheel's motion, rolling this ball and letting it spin away till it falls into a slot on the wheel. This slot determines the winning number and other payoffs.

After a winning number is determined, the dealer collects all the losing chips first, and then pays off the winning bets. After this is done, the players make bets prior to the next spin of the ball, and the whole procedure begins again.

There is usually a pitboss in the vicinity of the roulette wheel. He or she may supervise the play at the roulette table and will be called upon in case there is a dispute between the players and the dealer or if the players themselves disagree. But this rarely happens when all the players use different colored roulette chips.

Roulette Chips

As we mentioned, the chips are in different colors and are marked differently than other casino chips. A player can't wager them at any other game in the casino. Not only that, but players are forbidden from taking these chips away from the roulette table. When they've finished playing, they must turn in all their chips to the dealer, who will pay off the player by exchanging these for casino chips, which can then be brought to the cashier's cage and exchanged for cash.

There is usually a standard value placed on the roulette chips. In the old days, before inflation, 10¢ or 25¢ chips were the standard. Today, it's hard to find a standard chip value less than $1. If a player gives the dealer a $20 bill he or she will receive 20 chips, each having a standard value of $1. However, the player is not stuck with this value.

Suppose that a player came with a $100 bill and wanted each chip to be valued at $5. This will be done, and the dealer, to make certain that there is no mistake, will place that colored chip on the outside rim of the wheel with a $5 marker on it, or a button to show that a stack of 20 chips is worth $100.

Where no chips are on the rim, everyone is playing with the standard value chips. These chips will come in enough colors, usually eight or ten different ones, to accommodate that many players. There will also be enough chairs at the roulette table for this many players.

Players may change the valuation of their chips. If a player won a lot of money, rather than betting handfuls of $1 chips, he may change the valuation to $5 for his colored chips, by turning them in, and getting them re-valued, or getting different colored chips. He or she may not want to bet standard casino chips of that same valuation, since there may be a problem if another player is also betting casino chips, and there may be a dispute as to who is entitled to a payoff. The same holds true for cash bets, which we don't recommend using.

For bigger bets, casino chips of the regular kind can be used. This is for $5, $25 and $100 bets. However, the vast majority of bets will be made by using the roulette chips.

When payoffs are made, the dealer **cuts** the chips, that is, he breaks into the stacks of chips at his disposal. If the payoff is 17 chips, for example, he'll cut a 20 stack by taking away three chips from that stack and moving them by hand to the winner.

This is in contrast to the European game where a **rake** is used to collect and pay off chips. In both games, after the number has come up, some kind of marker is placed on the layout to indicate the winning number before the losing chips are collected and winning bets are paid off.

The American Wheel

The game of roulette depends on the spin of the wheel, an ornate device that is approximately three feet in diameter and contains slots numbered from 1 to 36, plus a 0 and 00.

The bowl of the wheel, which takes up most of the space on a roulette wheel contains numbered pockets. Above this are eight metal buffers, some horizontal and some vertical, which are there to slow down the ball as it spins counter to the wheel's motion, so that it will fall into a pocket in the most random manner possible.

When it falls into a pocket, that pocket corresponds to a particular number, and that number determines which bets win and which lose for that spin of the wheel.

Each pocket is separated from its neighbors by metal dividers, which are known as separators. As the ball slows down, it may fall into a pocket only to bounce up and into another pocket, but eventually its inertia will cause it to remain in one pocket. That pocket contains a number, and that's the winning number for that spin.

There are 36 numbers in all, half in black and half in red, plus two extra numbers, the 0 and 00, which are in green. The numbers aren't in consecutive order on the wheel, but are placed randomly, with red and black numbers alternating, except when broken up by the 0 and 00.

With thirty six numbers on the wheel, half will be odd and half even, half will be black and half red, and half will be in the lower tier (1-18) and half in the higher tier (19-36). All of these are possible bets; odd-even, red-black, and high-low, and as we shall see, are paid off at even-money.

If there were only 36 numbers, then the house would have no advantage over the player, and it would be merely a game of chance without either side, the bettor or casino, having an edge. However, the addition of the 0 and 00 gives the house a definite advantage of 5.26%. These could be called **house numbers,** because they are winning numbers for the house when the player bets on any of the even-money propositions just mentioned, as well as on other numbers and betting propositions.

A gambler could bet on the 0 and 00 as a number,

The American Wheel

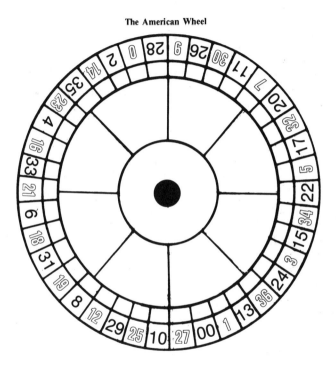

as well as any other numbers, but then it means that there are 38 possible numbers to bet on, with the payoff at 35-1 on a single number, still giving the casino a 5.26% advantage.

Since the house has a built-in advantage, it wants the game played as honestly as possible, and therefore the roulette wheels are built as friction-free as possible, so that there is no **bias** or deviation from a random situation prevailing. The wheels are inspected frequently and checked out for any worn parts, such as pockets or dividers, for these may create such a bias.

Some players go from wheel to wheel, clocking them and checking out the pattern of numbers that come up, hoping for such a bias, but it is rarely found. If more numbers come up in any sequence out of the ordinary, it is more probably coincidence, for when there's a random sampling, numbers can repeat and come up in strange sequences, and the spins can still be the result of chance.

The Roulette Layout

Now we come to the partner of the wheel at the roulette table, the layout. The layout contains all the possible betting situations that a player can have while playing roulette. The following is a typical roulette layout.

The layouts are usually in green. The numbers from 1 through 36 are divided into three columns,

		0	00	
1to18	1st 12	1	2	3
		4	5	6
EVEN		7	8	9
		10	11	12
◇	2nd 12	13	14	15
		16	17	18
◆		19	20	21
		22	23	24
ODD	3rd 12	25	26	27
		28	29	30
19to36		31	32	33
		34	35	36
		2-1	2-1	2-1

15

and are in numerical order. Each one is either red or black, corresponding to the colors on the wheel. 0 and 00 are at the head of the columns of numbers, and may be bet upon separately or together.

On the outside are the **even-money** bets, 1-18, Even, red, black, odd and 19-36. Between them and the columns are the **dozens bets**, 1-12, 13-24 and 25-36, placed so that they correspond with the numbers in the columns. On the layout these dozens bets are marked 1st 12, 2nd 12 and 3rd 12.

Finally we have the **columns bets**, which are at the far end of the columns, opposite the 0 and 00 areas. They each show 2-1, and are paid off at that price. Each of these column areas covers all the numbers running down the column.

This is the standard layout to be found in American casinos, and as we have said, it will accommodate all the possible bets that can be made at the game of roulette.

III. Inside Bets

The bets we'll be discussing in this section could be called **inside** bets, since they take place within the 1-36 numbers plus the 0 and 00. With the exception of one bet, the Five-Number bet, which gives the house a 7.89% advantage, all the following wagers in American roulette give the house an edge of 5.26%

Inside Bets

3	6	9	12	15	18	21	24	27	30	33	36
2	5	8	11	14	17	20	23	26	29	32	35
1	4	7	10	13	16	19	22	25	28	31	34

Let's begin with a favorite of roulette players the world over.

Straight-Up Bets

Single Number Bet — Pays 35-1.

When a chip is placed on a single number, as shown on the layout with a chip placed in number 3, this is known as a straight-up wager, and if the number comes up, the payoff is 35-1. If any other number comes up, including 0 and 00, the bet is lost.

Straight-Up Bets

A single number bet can be made on any number on the layout, including numbers 1-36, plus 0 and 00. No matter what number he places the chip on, the payoff will be the same, at 35-1.

A player is not limited to one straight-up bet. He may make as many as he desires, and place as many chips on a single number (up to the house limit) as he or she desires. For example, a player can put five chips on number 0, two on number 4, and one each on numbers 12, 15, 23 and 34. It is up to the inclinations of the player. No one will object, and since your chips will have a special roulette color, they'll easily be identified as yours, and you'll be paid off.

To bet correctly, place your chip in the center of the numbered box, being careful not to touch any of the surrounding lines. If you touch the lines, you might have another kind of bet.

If another bettor likes your number and has

placed a chip in that box, that doesn't foreclose you from making the same bet. Simply place your chip on the bettor's chip. Or you may place several chips on the bettor's chip. This is perfectly valid. The house edge on this bet is 5.26%.

Split Bets

Two-Number Bet — Pays 17-1.

In order to make a split bet, you should place your chip on the line between two contiguous or adjacent numbers. On the layout, we see the chip placed between numbers 6 and 9 as a split bet, covering both numbers. Also, the chip between 5 and 6 is a split bet.

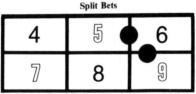

Split Bets

If either number comes up on a split bet, the player wins at 17-1. Split bets give the player double the chance to win, at half the payoff. Any two numbers may be split, as long as there is a line separating them. In addition, 0 and 00 may be bet as a split number, either by putting a chip between these numbers, or putting one on the line between the second and third dozens, when a player can't reach the 0 and 00 box.

Trio Bets

Three Number Bet   Pays 11-1.

A trio bet can be made by placing a chip on the line separating the dozens betting area from the columns of numbers. Thus, the chip on the number 13 line on the layout will cover the numbers 13, 14 and 15.

Trio Bets

When making a trio bet, the player will have three consecutive numbers covered, and will be paid 11-1 if any of those numbers come up on the wheel.

As you can see by the layout, the numbers that can be covered with a trio bet include 1, 2 and 3; 10, 11 and 12; 25, 26 and 27, to show but three other examples.

The house advantage on this bet is still 5.26%.

Corner Bets

Four-Number Bet   Pays 8-1.

This bet is made when a chip is placed at the point where all four numbers converge, right in that corner, as the chip placed between numbers 23, 24, 26 and 27 shows. Now, if any of those numbers come up on the next spin of the wheel, the payoff will be 8-1. This is a pretty versatile wager and can be used to cover various groups of four numbers, such as 2, 3, 5 and 6; 7, 8, 10 and 11; 22, 23, 25 and 26; 32, 33, 35 and 36, as examples.

Corner Bets

The corner bet gives the house the usual 5.26% advantage.

Five-Number Bet

Five-Numbers Bet   Pays 6-1.

This wager can only be made one way, and it covers the numbers, 0, 00, 1, 2, and 3. It is made by placing the chip at the outer corner of the line separating the 0 and 1 as shown in the diagram. However, after noting where the chip goes, forget about this bet, for one very good reason. It gives the house an advantage of 7.89%, and is the **worst bet** on the entire roulette layout.

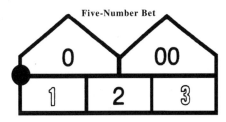

Five-Number Bet

Since the French wheel, which contains only 0, doesn't have the 00, this bet can't be made on that wheel. So, remember our advice, and never make a five-number bet on the American wheel.

Six-Number Bet

Six-Numbers   Pays 5-1.

As we can see from the layout diagram, the chip for this wager should be placed on the outside line separating the dozens bets from the inside numbers, at a point where this line crosses a line perpendicular to it, separating the six numbers we want to bet on.

Six-Number Bet

In the diagram, this chip is placed so that the numbers 28, 29, 30, 31, 32 and 33 are covered. Thus one chip covers all six numbers, and if any of the numbers hit, then the bet will be paid off at 5-1.

There are eleven possible ways to make this six-number bet running up and down the side of the layout. Since it covers so many numbers at one time, with a good 5-1 payoff, it's a popular bet.

The house edge on this wager is 5.26%.

A final note on these wagers: No matter how they're made and for how many chips, if the five-number wager is avoided, then the house edge will never be more nor less than 5.26%.

With all of these wagers, the player may make several bets of the same kind, covering several numbers, and combinations of bets, covering as many numbers as he or she wishes, with as many chips as he or she desires to bet, provided that it is within the house limit on wagers.

IV. Outside Bets

The bets we'll now cover take place outside the 1-36 and 0, 00 numbered area, and are therefore considered **outside wagers.**

There are three types of bets here. First there are the even-money wagers, then the dozens bets and finally the column bets. We'll discuss each in turn.

Outside Bets

1st 12		2nd 12		3rd 12	
1to18	EVEN	◇	◆	ODD	19to36

24

The Even-Money Bets

There are three possible types of bets that can be made at even-money; high-low, odd-even or red-black. Of course, a player can make wagers on each of these choices, betting, for example, odd, red and high.

1 to 18	EVEN	◇	◆	ODD	19 to 36

When betting on even-money choices, the house wins automatically if the ball lands in the 0 or 00. There's one exception to this, and this takes place in Atlantic City, or wherever else there's a **surrender** rule.

Let's discuss this now. If the number coming up is 0 or 00, where surrender is allowed, the casino will allow you to remove **one-half of your bet**. In other words, you're surrendering half your bet.

In the European casinos they go one step further. In those casinos, there is the **en prison** rule. You can either surrender half your bet, or allow your bet to be **imprisoned for one more spin.** If your choice then comes up, your bet stays intact. You won't win but at least you have your bet back. In Atlantic City you just get surrender, however.

In the Nevada casinos, neither rule is in force. So, if you bet on any even-money choice and the 0 or 00 comes up, you're out of luck. You lose your chip or chips outright.

High-Low Bets

The first of the even-money bets we'll discuss is high-low. You can bet high (19-36) or low (1-18). If you bet high and any number from 19 to 36 comes up, you win your bet at even-money, or 1-1. If you bet low and any number from 1-18 comes up, you win that bet, also at even-money.

High-Low Bet

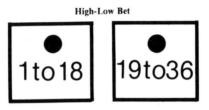

Odd-Even

If you bet odd, then if any odd number comes up on the next spin of the wheel, you win your wager at even-money, or 1-1. If you bet even, then if any even number comes up, you bet is paid off at even-money. Remember, however, that the numbers 0 and 00 are losers for this kind of bet, as they are for all even-money bets.

Odd-Even Bet

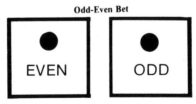

Red-Black

There are 18 red numbers and 18 black numbers, so the chances of a red or black number coming up on the next spin of the wheel are equal. If you bet on red, then you will be paid off at even-money, or 1-1 if a red number comes up. If you bet black, then you win if a black number comes up at even-money.

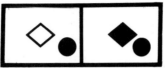

The layout diagram shows where you make your wagers for these even-money choices. You can bet any amount up to the house limit, which is usually higher for even-money choices than for the inside numbers, because the payoff is only at even-money.

These even-money choices are the heart of many roulette systems, and we'll cover a few in the later sections of this book, showing how they work, as well as their pitfalls.

Dozens Bets

These bets are paid off at 2-1, and there are three ways to bet them. You can bet on the first dozen, the second dozen or the third dozen. The first dozen covers numbers from 1-12 and is often called on layouts, the **1st 12**. The numbers from 13-24 is the second dozen and is known as the **2nd 12**. Finally the third dozen, from 25-36 is known as the **3rd 12**. For each of those bets, you are covering 12 numbers. Some players bet on two dozens at one time, giving themselves 24 numbers. But on these bets, as on the even-number wagers and the columns wagers, the house edge is always 5.26%.

1st 12 ●	2nd 12 ●	3rd 12 ●

When a 0 or 00 comes up, you have an automatic loser. These numbers aren't included in the dozens bets, and there is no surrender or *en prison* rule covering them in any casino.

The layout diagram shows just how to make these wagers, and where to place the chip or chips you bet. The house limit on these bets is higher than those on the inside numbers.

Columns Bet

These bets are made at the head of each column directly opposite on the layout from 0 and 00. A bet on a particular column covers 12 numbers, some red and some black.

Columns Bet

3	6	9	12	15	18	21	24	27	30	33	36	2-1 ●
2	5	8	11	14	17	20	23	26	29	32	35	2-1 ●
1	4	7	10	13	16	19	22	25	28	31	34	2-1 ●

The payoff is at 2-1 for each column bet, but the 0 and 00 aren't included in any column. If they come up, the column bet is lost, for there is no surrender or *en prison* rule on column wagers.

The house edge is 5.26% on all column bets.

We have discussed previously the *en prison* and surrender rules on even-money wagers. The house edge without these rules is 5.26% on even-money and on the dozens and columns bets. With the *en prison* and surrender rules, the house advantage drops to 2.70% **only on the even-money wagers**.

Chart 1
Recapitulation of Bets and Payoffs

Single Number	35-1
Two Numbers	17-1
Three Numbers	11-1
Four Numbers	8-1
Five Numbers	6-1
Six Numbers	5-1
Column	2-1
Dozen	2-1
Odd-Even *	1-1
Red-Black *	1-1
High-Low *	1-1

All of the above bets give the house an advantage of 5.26%, except for the five-numbers bet, which gives the casino an advantage of 7.89%.

* When the surrender feature is allowed, the house advantage on these bets drops to 2.70%.

V. European Roulette

The European game and the American game are nearly the same. The main difference, besides the use of French terms, is in the use of but a single zero in the European game, while the American wheel has a zero and a double zero. There is also the **en prison** rule used in the European game. Both the **en prison** rule and the single zero are beneficial to the players, and bring the casino advantage down to 1.35%.

The following is a French wheel:

The French Wheel

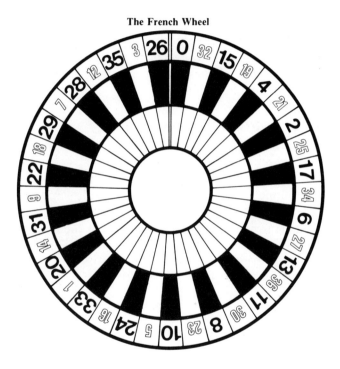

This wheel has spaces for 37 numbers, the numerals 1-36 and the 0. Red and black numbers alternate, but the placement of numbers is different than the American wheel.

Like the American wheel, there is a groove near the rim of the wheel where the croupier places the ball, spinning it counter to the action of the wheel, to give it the most random kind of spin. Then it hits metal buffers as it loses velocity, and finally falls into one of the pockets, which is separated from the other pockets by metal sides.

The Layout

The following is a French layout used in the European and English casinos.

It differs from the American layout in that the even money choices are on opposite sides, and the dozens bets can be made on two different sides. The wheel is to the top of the box showing the 0.

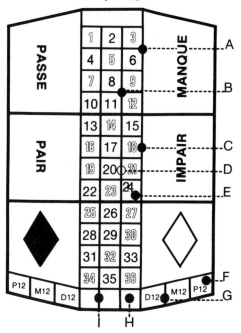

The European Layout

The European Layout

A. Transversale	6	numbers.
B. Carre	4	numbers.
C. Transversale	3	numbers.
D. Cheval	2	numbers.
E. Number, *en plein*	1	number.
F. Dozen	12	numbers.
G. Two dozens	24	numbers.
H. Column	12	numbers.
I. Two columns	24	numbers.

Let's compare the European and American bets, showing the different nomenclature.

Chart 2		
European and American Nomenclature		
American Bet	**French Term**	**Odds**
Straight-Up (One Number)	En plein	35-1
Split (Two Numbers)	A cheval	17-1
Trio (Three Numbers)	Transversale	11-1
Corner (Four Numbers)	Carre	8-1
Six Numbers	Sixain	5-1
* Red-Black	Rouge-Noir	1-1
* High-Low	Passe-Manque	1-1
* Odd-Even	Impair-Pair	1-1
Column	Colonne	2-1
Dozen	Douzaine	2-1

* The *en prison* rule is in effect for these betting choices only.

When making the dozen bets, you should realize that the first dozen (1-12) is marked as **P12** on the layout, standing for **Premiere**. The second dozen (13-24) is called **M12** for **Moyenne** meaning middle. The third dozen is **D12** for **Derniere**, or last.

The *en prison* rule can be summarized as follows: When a 0 comes up on the wheel, the player's bet isn't lost. He or she has two choices. First, he or she can surrender half the wager made, which is known as **partage**, and take off the other half of the bet. Or the bet can be imprisoned for another spin and if it wins, then the bet is whole, but nothing else is won. To differentiate this wager from the ordinary wager, the chip or chips are placed on the line that borders the betting area.

Since the house advantage with the *en prison* rule is 1.35%, the most advantageous bets for the players would be on the even-money choices when playing in a European casino.

There are many special bets available at European casinos, mostly involving what the French call **voisins**, or neighbors. These can be the *voisins* of any particular number on the wheel, which includes the number and two numbers on either side, making it a five-chip bet.

There is the **voisins du zero**, which is a nine-chip bet, with eight chips bet on splits and one chip on the trio, 0-2-3.

There are other wagers that are special to the European wheel, such as **finals, les tiers** and **les orphelins**, which are rather complicated. We would advise the player to concentrate instead on the even-money choices and the simpler bets, such as corner bets or splits.

VI. Strategies and Systems at Roulette

Because of the high house edge at the American wheel without the surrender rule (5.26%) this is not a game that you might want to play for very serious money. The house advantage is very strong and quite difficult to overcome in the long run.

Therefore, limit your losses, and if you find yourself winning, try to make a good score and then quit winners. That kind of philosophy can't be beat when gambling.

Getting Your Roulette Chips

When you come to the table, you should first inquire of the dealer just what the minimum bets are at the table. If they're too high for your pocketbook, then don't play at that table. **Don't gamble with money you can't afford to lose, either financially or emotionally.**

Different casinos have different minimum bet limits. And they have different standard valuations for their chips. Some casinos will have a 25¢ value as a standard value. This means that a stack of 20 chips will cost you $5. This is the way to figure out the basic valuations; find out what a stack of chips will cost you.

Some casinos will have 50¢, $1 or even higher valuations placed on their chips. At 50¢ a chip, a stack will cost you $10. $1 chips will set you back $20 for a stack of 20 chips.

If you feel comfortable with the amount of money you're going to risk, then the next question you want to ask the dealer is this: What is the minimum bet allowed for the inside as well as the outside numbers. The inside numbers are all those numbers, from 1-36 plus the 0 and 00, that can be bet as one, two, three, four or six number bets. The outside bets are those that pay off at even-money, plus the dozen and column wagers.

Even though the chips cost 25¢ each, the casino might require a minimum outside bet of $1, and an inside minimum bet of 25¢ on any choice but with at least four chips in play at one time. In other words, you can't just place down one chip on an inside betting proposition. You'll have to put down at least four on one or several betting choices and that means risking a dollar.

This is fairly standard in casinos. So make certain that your bankroll can handle it. If you're at a table with a $1 valuation for the chips, and you must bet four (and sometimes five) chips at one time on the inside propositions, then with a few losses you're going to be out of your original stake.

What Bets to Make

If you're playing at a standard American table, with the 0 and 00 and no surrender, then all your bets will give the house the same advantage of 5.26%. That is, except for the five-number wager (0, 00, 1, 2 and 3) which we don't advise making.

The higher the odds, the less likely you'll win. The lower the odds, the more often you'll have wins. Thus, if you bet only on single numbers as straight-up bets, you'll get 35-1 for a win, but the odds are 37-1 against this happening.

On the other hand, if you bet on the even-money choices, the odds against winning on these are only 20-18 against. You have 18 numbers working for you, but 20 against you, including the 0 and 00. Obviously you will theoretically win 18 out of 38 times, much better than 1 out of 37 times when betting a straight-up number.

However, the payoff is much less, only even-money. Therefore, you must use your discretion when making bets. Are you the type that wants to take a shot at a big payoff, or do you want to conserve your betting capital and hope to get a little ahead? It's your choice; the odds are the same as far as house percentage goes.

There are ways to compromise. You can make six-number bets and cover a large variety of numbers and still get a good payoff. You can bet a key number, and bet it straight-up, surrounding it with corner and trio bets. All kinds of possibilities are available at the roulette table. Again, the choice is yours.

When playing at a table that allows surrender, then by all means concentrate on the even-money betting propositions. They cut the house edge in half, and why not take advantage of this? The same holds true when betting in a European game. Bet on the even-money choices. You get a second chance at winning back your bet when a 0 shows. And the house edge on this bet is down to 1.35%.

Betting Systems

The most well-known, and the most treacherous systems to play are the Martingale and the Grand Martingale. The Martingale is often played by novices who feel that sooner or later their choice is going to come up, and to rationalize their bets, they call upon the *law of averages*.

Here's how the Martingale system works. It's really nothing more than a doubling up system. After a loss, you double your bet till you win. For example, let's suppose you bet $1. You lose. Then you bet $2. You lose. You bet $4. You lose. You bet $8 and win.

Having won, you start all over again with a $1 wager. How much can you win with this system? Well, when you finish a sequence of doubling up with a win, you are ahead $1 only. Here's why.

Bet	Loss
$1	$1
$2	$3
$4	$7

At this point, you're behind $7. Then you bet $8 and win, and so you're ahead $1. Even if the bets escalate to $16, $32, $64 $128 and $256, when you finally win, you win $1. Imagine betting $256 to win $1! But that's what this system is all about.

The Grand Martingale is even tougher. After each loss you add a unit to the bet, so that you win more than $1 when you finally win. But the loss sequence is $1, $3, $7, $15 and so forth, and this can lead to astronomical losses in a very short time. Avoid this system as well.

The systems players who are die-hards think that the doubling up method will win because of the law of averages. So, after they've lost five bets on red, they feel red is overdue because of the *law of averages*.

What they don't know is that there is no law of averages. There is the law of large numbers, which roughly states that the more events played the closer to the theoretical norm will be the result.

Thus, at the time the systems player is hoping for red to come up, he doesn't know that after a million spins of the wheel (excluding the 0 and 00) red has come up 521,202 and black has come up 478,798 and black still has a long way to go to catch up. It may never catch up, but will come closer to the 50% norm as time goes by, and there are several more million spins of the wheel.

If you want to play a betting system, play a very conservative one. For example, you might bet $1 and if it loses, bet $2. If that loses, you just want to get even, so you bet $3. If that loses, you've lost $6 and stop, and start again with a $1 bet, hoping to win enough times during the first two spins to make up for the loss. Of course, you're not going to get rich that way. But you won't be losing your bankroll with one bad run of luck.

Since roulette is a leisurely game where you can sit down comfortably and make bets between spins of the wheel without much pressure, we'd sugggest that you buy two stacks of chips and have fun playing, hoping by luck to make some money.

Therefore, our best advice would be to play some favorite numbers, make some corner bets and perhaps a few even-number wagers. Enjoy yourself. With some luck, you could win big.

VII. Money Management

This is always important in gambling. It means managing your gambling stake so that it not only can last a long time, but will give you the chance of winning. For purposes of playing roulette, we'd suggest getting two stacks of chips only if you can afford to take this risk. Play with the standard valuations. Now you have 40 chips to bet. To make them last, you might pick a few favorite numbers and cover them with corner or six-number bets, to give yourself a good chance of picking up a winning number. At the same time, place a chip on two favorite numbers. If they hit, you're getting 35-1.

Try and double your stake. If you do that, you're doing well at roulette. You've made a nice win, and it's time to leave the table. If your luck turns the other way and you lose, then don't reach into your pocket for more cash. Set your loss limits when you sit down at the table. Two stacks and that's all you'll lose.

In this way, you'll have a shot at winning some money, have some fun gambling, and it won't cost you that much if you lose.

Good luck!

XIII. More Winning Approaches

Bias of Wheels

Although, as we have shown, the game is one of pure chance governed by the **law of averages**, it is possible that some wheels may have a bias. By **bias**, we mean that there is something wrong with the wheel itself or with the mechanism of the wheel.

For example, the wheel may not be perfectly placed on a table, so that it tilts to one side ever so slightly, so slightly that the human eye can't detect this. But what happens is that the ball finds its way disproportionately into certain numbers more frequently. This can happen, especially in casinos where sloppy procedures in placing the wheel have been used.

Another bias may be found in the metal buffers which might get worn and will slow the ball down in other ways than pure chance. Or certain pockets might be worn and thus more receptive to the ball.

After all, this is a device that is manufactured to certain exacting standards, but those standards may not hold up to the damage that repeated use of the wheel might inflict. Personnel in casinos can get sloppy, and not continually test the machine. Instead, the bias will continue.

If you are playing roulette at one of these machines, and you detect any such bias, then by all means take advantage of it.

You may see something or may feel that certain numbers come up more than others, in a way that goes against the law of large numbers.

A Bias Story

A habitue of the game told me that he was playing in a small casino in France and noticed that, under the glare of the chandelier, a few of the metal pockets gleamed unnaturally. They seemed to be more worn than others, and he clocked the wheel for an hour while making inconsequential wagers on the even-money choices.

Those worn pockets were attracting the ball more often than the other numbers, and he gradually started to make big bets on the four numbers that he had detected in this manner. He was rewarded with a large profit for the evening.

He returned the next evening with the same good results. He made money for five straight nights, very serious money, and was dismayed to find that on the sixth night, the wheel had been replaced with a new one. Some executive of the casino had noticed something and replaced it.

My friend took the next plane back to London.

Winning Streaks

Although roulette is theoretically a game of pure chance, in which skill plays no part, there are times when everything seems to go the gambler's way.

When this happens, it is wise to take advantage of this rush and increase your wagers.

Although most of the time you have to guess which numbers to play, or you simply play favorite numbers, there are other times when you can visualize what is going to happen. It rarely happens, but it does happen.

Whether it's ESP or some other kind of psychic intuition, the point is, it does happen. I can recall such a situation in a London casino.

A Roulette Bonanza

I had arrived in London a few day earlier, and as a newcomer, you cannot simply go into a casino and gamble. The British authorities, in their purported wisdom, have a tight rule. You must show your passport to gain admittance, and then must wait for 48 hours to play.

The rule is supposedly there to prevent a visitor to their fair country from impulsively gambling the moment he hits a casino. It seems to be a strange rule, for the same person impulsively gambles 48 hours later. But that's another story altogether.

I waited for 48 hours, which amounted really to two days and then went to this casino near Soho in the West End of London. It was a crowded smoky place, filled for the most part with foreigners, most of them Oriental or Asian. There were roulette wheels and blackjack tables.

I liked the European game of roulette with its en prison rule and single zero, and had done well in the past, so I decided to try my luck. I played for a few hours and won a little bit of money, about 50 pounds, then returned to my hotel at Knightsbridge, near Harrod's.

The next day, I started talking to a lovely nurse who was from New Zealand, and who, like me, had just arrived a few days before in London. We made a date for dinner that evening, and after a sumptuous Chinese meal, I invited her to the gambling club for a bit of roulette.

At the club, she could enter without the 48 hour restriction as my guest, since I was now a *bona fide* member of the gambling establishment. We went to a roulette table after exchanging some pounds for chips.

I started with fifty pounds, my win the other night. I bet on some even-money choices and the table was choppy. I would win, lose, win and then lose, and in all I was down about five pounds when Alice, who now knew the game from my explanations and her observations, told me to make a bet on 29.

"Why?" I asked.

"I just have a feeling."

I bet three pounds on the number and was rewarded as the croupier called out **vingt et neuf, noir, impair,** that is, 29, black and odd. I had won 105 pounds on the bet, and now hesitated. I took off the three pound bet and waited as the wheel spun around and the dealer placed the ball on the wheel.

"33," Alice cried.

I bet five pounds on 33. 12 won.

"Bet 33 again," she said, "I just have this feeling. So I bet another give pounds on 33, and it came up. 175 pounds was the payoff. I had now a net profit from her choice of 275 pounds.

I didn't make a bet for the next three spins, then Alice told me to bet 14. I bet it and lost 10 pounds, bet again and lost another 10 pounds, and again lost 10 pounds.

However, on the fourth try, I was rewarded with a win. 14 had come up. 350 pounds was the win.

"How do you know what numbers to bet?" I asked her, as I stacked the chips in front of me.

" I just have this feeling."

"And you've never played roulette before?"

"Never, but sometimes I just feel things."

"Like what?" I asked.

"Play 9," she suddenly said. It came up five rolls later. And then I won again with 10, which she predicted.

Then the next number, 36 didn't come up, and after six futile bets, she suddenly said, "let's get out of here. I can't stand to be in here anymore."

I cashed in and found that I had won 1,400 pounds. An amazing win in just over an hour's play, in which I hadn't even picked a number on my own.

"I could feel it leaving. It won't come back there anymore."

"What do you mean? You won't go back to the casino with me?"

"No, not me. It won't come back."

"What is it" I asked.

"It's hard to explain. It's just something...." Her voice trailed off. "It was there and now it's gone. I can't really explain."

I'll always remember the "Kiwi" with the magical powers who made all that money for me in that London casino.

IX. Clocking the Numbers

Using Pen and Pad

When playing roulette, it's a good idea to go to the table with a pen and pad, and keep track of the numbers as they come up on the wheel. In most casinos, that's the only way you can know which numbers have hit previously.

In one of the newer Strip hotels in Las Vegas, there's an automatic screen which lists the previous 16 numbers. You may find this screen in other casinos, and the numbers shown are a big help to the player.

A Roulette Story

I recently clocked the numbers there and was not so surprised to find that three numbers had repeated in the last thirty six number cycle. This may have been due to pure chance, or possibly a bias in the wheel, which is a real long shot.

Or it may have come from the habits of the croupier himself, who spun the ball at a certain speed and began his spin in various places, favoring some over others. Or the metal separators may have gotten worn from use, trapping the ball.

There was no instant way to find out, but I started betting on the numbers that had come up more than once. There were three of these numbers; 11, 24 and 31.

Clocking a 36 Game Cycle

Here's what I found: In the next 36 game cycle, the 11 came up three more times, and the 24 twice again, and the 27 just once.

By betting a dollar on these three numbers, I grossed $210. My losses were $102, giving me a net of $108. Not bad at all. Now, I noticed that 28 had also come up twice, as did 6. So I changed my pattern of betting to now bet 6, 11, 24 and 28, saying adieu to the 27.

The 11 came up one more time, the 28 once more, and both the 6 and 24 missed altogether. The 27 came up once again, but I didn't have it. So, for the next 36 spins of the wheel, my gross win was $70, while I lost $142, for a net loss of $72.

I now studied the screen, which was, in reality, two separate columns of numbers placed above the table. The 11 and 28 had hit, as had the 27, which I lost faith in, and the 30 was now active, with two wins. So, for the next cycle, I bet a dollar on all these numbers. I was going with the flow.

I was rewarded. Good old 11 hit once, 27 hit twice more, 28 missed, but 30 was still hot, hitting twice in a row. Something was going on definitely with the 30. Now, at the end of that cycle of 36 spins, I had grossed $175, while dropping $139, for a net win of $36. At that point, I called it a day, and added up my totals.

Gross wins: $455.
Gross losses: $383.
Net win: $72.

Not bad for a wheel with two zeros. I now decided to look around for another wheel in another casino. I skipped the Strip hotels and found myself downtown, playing at a casino which shall remain nameless.

This one had no screen listing the previous wins of particular numbers, so I clocked them myself, betting a slight progression on red and black to pass the time and give myself something to root for.

Clocking a 40 Game Cycle

I clocked forty numbers and decided that would be my cycle. In the first forty number cycle, 10 hit three times, 17 twice and the rest were single wins, except for 00, which hit three times, rather spoiling my progression. So, I was ready.

I decided to bet $2 on each of these numbers, 00, 10 and 17. In the next forty roll cycle, the 00 stayed hot, hitting twice, and the 17 also hit twice, while the 10 hit once, but the 36, which I didn't have, hit four times.

So at the end of forty spins, I toted up my numbers. I had grossed $350. I had lost $235, for a net win of $115.

I now studied the wheel closely while it was in spin. The room was rather dark, but I could see that certain metal pockets retained more of a shine than others, glinting a reflection off some distant light. Maybe they were more worn, who knows? I put my money where my instincts were.

I now bet $3 on 00, 10, 17 and added 36 to my little group. I was ready for another 40 spin cycle. For the first thirty rolls nothing happened.

I didn't hit once, and at $12 a pop, I was already down $360 for this wretched cycle. I decided, instead of quitting, to give it the ten more spins the cycle deserved. 00 came up, then 36, and right back to 00.

Then, after five misses, 00 hit again, as did 36 right afterwards. I was really onto something. At this point, I had grossed, during this cycle, the sum of $525. My losses were $465, for a win of $60.

So far, so good. I looked over my notepad. 18

had hit twice as had 19 and 25.

I decided to go all out for the next forty cycles of spins.

Taking a deep breath, I resolved to bet $5 per number. By this time a small crowd had gathered, for anytime a player hits numbers it looks exciting. I was betting pure numbers, not hedging the bets at all, and the payoffs looked good, with $25 chips being paid off.

My numbers were now 00, 36, and adding to these I put down 18, 19 and 25. At $5 a pop, I was betting $25 each time the wheel spun around. At forty spins, that would be $1,000 down the drain if I didn't hit anything. Of course, each win was $175, and if I hit 6 times I'd be ahead.

We were off! The first six spins gave me nothing, then the good old 00 hit. And then, like clockwork, the 36 hit right afterwards. In the course of the forty spins, I hit four more times, twice with 18, once with 19 and once more with 36.

So I hit six times in the forty spins, giving me a gross win of $1,050. My losses were $970, for a net win of $80.

I was a bit washed up, but happy to be ahead for the session.

40 Game Cycle Win Analysis

Later, over coffee, I figured out what my chances

were to win. In the simplest terms, if I played a forty number cycle, I was investing $1,000, by betting five numbers at $5 a shot.

I therefore had to win 5.714 times to break even, and since there was no such odd number of times to win at roulette, in reality, I needed six wins to come out ahead, which was what happened.

If I had bet four numbers, again at $5 a pop, it would cost me $800 for the full 40 spin cycle. With each win determined at $175 ($35 x 5) I would have to win a theoretical 4.57 times to break even.

I calculated this down to a $1 bet. Still sticking with the 40 cycle spin, to comes out as follows:

Numbers Bet	Wins Needed to Break Even
One	1.14
Two	2.28
Three	3.42
Four	4.57
Five	5.71
Six	6.85

In reality, each additional number bet has to win by a multiple of 1.14 in a forty spin cycle to break even (actually, to be very slightly ahead.)

Summary

I felt comfortable clocking the numbers and

betting accordingly. I came out ahead in each session I played, and my luck has continued. I highly recommend this play rather than a random selection of numbers to bet.

It gives you a slight edge over other methods, especially if the croupier, wheel or something else is slightly out of whack, causing certain numbers to come up with more frequency than others.

Roulette Tradition

Once you understand the game, and have the necessary funds, you can play the game anywhere it is legal to play.

That is one of the beauties of roulette. It has attracted gamblers from the anonymous to the great. Winston Churchill loved to play roulette on the French Riviera and in Monte Carlo. When interviewed late in his great and illustrious life, he was asked if he had any regrets. His answer was succinct.

"Yes," the great leader replied, "I should have played red more often."

Thus, when you play roulette, you're following in the steps of many great personages who have been attracted and fascinated by this wonderful game.

VIII. Glossary

American Wheel—The roulette wheel containing a 0 and 00.

Ball—The white ball used in roulette, which is made of plastic, spun against the wheel's rotation to give a random spin.

Column Bet—A bet on one of the three columns on the roulette layout, each of which contains 12 numbers, and is paid off at 2-1.

Combination Bet—A wager such as a corner bet, covering several numbers on the inside with the use of one chip.

Corner Bet—An inside bet using one chip to cover four numbers at one time. Also known as a **Four-Numbers Bet.**

Croupier—The French term for the employee who runs the roulette game.

Double Zero—See **Zero**.

Dozen Bet—A wager on either the first, second, or third dozen numbers on the layout.

En Prison Rule—When a 0 or 00 comes up, the player has the option of giving up half his bet or imprisoning the bet for one more spin. If the player's choice comes up then, the bet is not lost.

Even-Money Choices—Bets paid off at even-money, which include **High-Low, Odd-Even,** and **Red-Black**.

Five-Number Bet—A wager covering the 0, 00, 1, 2 and 3 which pays off at 6-1 and gives the house an advantage of 7.89%.

French Wheel—The standard wheel used in Europe containing but a single zero.

High-Low Bet—An even-money bet that the next spin will come up either high (19-36) or low (1-18), depending on whether the bettor has wagered on high or low.

Inside Bet—A wager on any of the numbers, or combinations of the numbers, including 0 and 00.

Layout—The printed surface showing all the wagers that can be made in roulette, on which players place their bets.

Martingale System—A doubling up system after each loss.

Odd-Even Bet—An even-money wager that the next spin will come up the way the player bet it, either an odd or even number.

Outside Bet—A wager on either the dozens, columns or even-money choices.

Red-Black Bet—A wager paid off at even-money on either the red or black numbers.

Six-Numbers Bet—A bet covering six inside numbers with one chip.

Split Bet—A bet covering two numbers with one chip, paying off at 17-1.

Straight-Up Bet—A wager on one particular number on the layout, which pays off at 35-1.

Trio Bet—An inside bet covering three numbers at one time with one chip.

Voisons—The French term for neighbors, referring to neighboring numbers on the French wheel.

Zero, Double Zero—Numbers on the wheel in addition to the regular 1-36 numerals, which allow the casino to have an edge over the players.

60

Baccarat Master Card Counter
NEW WINNING STRATEGY!

For the **first time**, Gambling Research Institute releases the **latest winning techniques** at baccarat. This **exciting** strategy, played by big money players in Monte Carlo and other exclusive locations, is based on principles that have made insiders and pros **hundreds of thousands of dollars** counting cards at blackjack - card counting!

NEW WINNING APPROACH

This brand **new** strategy now applies card counting to baccarat to give you a **new winning approach,** and is designed so that any player, with just a little effort, can successfully take on the casinos at their own game - and win!

SIMPLE TO USE, EASY TO MASTER

You learn how to count cards for baccarat without the mental effort needed for blackjack! No need to memorize numbers - keep the count on the scorepad. Easy-to-use, play the strategy while enjoying the game!

LEARN WHEN TO BET BANKER, WHEN TO BET PLAYER

No longer will you make bets on hunches and guesses - use the GRI Baccarat Master Card Counter to determine when to bet Player and when to bet Banker. You learn the basic counts (running and true), deck favorability, when to increase bets and much more in this **winning strategy**.

LEARN TO WIN IN JUST ONE SITTING

That's right! After **just one sitting** you'll be able to successfully learn this powerhouse strategy and use it to your advantage at the baccarat table. Be the best baccarat player at the table - the one playing the odds to **win**! Baccarat can be beaten. The Master Card Counter shows you how!

FREE BONUS!

Order now to receive **absolutely free**, The Basics of Winning Baccarat. One quick reading with this great primer shows you how to play and win.

To order, send $50 by bank check or money order to:
Cardoza Publishing.P.O. Box 1500, Cooper Station, New York, NY 10276

Win at Blackjack Without Counting Cards!

Breakthrough in Blackjack!!!
The Cardoza 1,2,3 Non-Counter Strategy

Beat Multiple Deck Blackjack Without Counting Cards!

You heard right! Now, for the **first time** ever, **win** at multiple deck black-jack **without counting cards**! Until I developed the Cardoza Multiple Deck Non-Counter (The 1,2,3 Strategy), I thought it was impossible. Don't be intimidated anymore by 4, 6 or 8 deck games - now *you* have the **advantage**!

Exciting Strategy - Anyone Can Win!

We're **excited** about this strategy for it allows anyone at all to **have the advantage** over any casino in the world in a multiple deck game. You don't need a great memory, you don't count cards, you don't need to be good at math - you only need to know the **winning secrets** of the Cardoza Multiple Deck Non-Counter and use but a **little effort** to be a **winner**.

Simple But Effective - Be a Leisurely Winner!

This strategy is so **simple**, yet so **effective**, you will be amazed. With a **minimum of effort**, this remarkable strategy, which we also call the 1,2,3 (as easy as 1,2,3), allows you to **win** without studiously following cards. Drink, converse, whatever - they'll never suspect that you can **beat the casino**!

Not as powerful as a card counting strategy, but **powerful enough to make you a winner** - with the odds!!!

Extra Bonus!

Complete listing of all options and variations at blackjack and how they affect the player. ($5 Value!) **Extra, Extra Bonus!!** Not really a bonus for we could not sell you the strategy without protecting you against getting barred. The 1,000 word essay, "How to Disguise the Fact That You're an Expert," and 1,500 word "How Not To Get Barred," are also included free. ($15 Value!)

To Order, send ~~$75~~ $50 by check or money order to <u>Cardoza Publishing</u>

PROFESSIONAL VIDEO POKER STRATEGY
Win at Video Poker - With the Odds!

At last, for the **first time,** and for **serious players only**, the GRI **Professional Video Poker** strategy is released so you too can play to win! **You read it right** - this strategy gives you the **mathematical advantage** over the casino and what's more, it's **easy to learn!**

PROFESSIONAL STRATEGY SHOWS YOU HOW TO WIN WITH THE ODDS
This **powerhouse strategy,** played for **big profits** by an **exclusive** circle of **professionals**, people who make their living at the machines, is now made available to you! You too can win - with the odds - and this **winning strategy** shows you how!

HOW TO PLAY FOR A PROFIT
You'll learn the **key factors** to play on a **pro level**: which machines will turn you a profit, break-even and win rates, hands per hour and average win per hour charts, time value, team play and more! You'll also learn big play strategy, alternate jackpot play, high and low jackpot play and key strategies to follow.

WINNING STRATEGIES FOR ALL MACHINES
This **comprehensive, advanced pro package** not only shows you how to win money at the 8-5 progressives, but also, the **winning strategies** for 10s or better, deuces wild, joker's wild, flat-top, progressive and special options features.

BE A WINNER IN JUST ONE DAY
In just one day, after learning our strategy, you will have the skills to **consistently win money** at video poker - with the odds. The strategies are easy to use under practical casino conditions.

BONUS - PROFESSIONAL PROFIT EXPECTANCY FORMULA ($15 VALUE)
For serious players, we're including this bonus essay which discusses the profit expectancy principles of video poker and how to relate them to real dollars and cents in your game.

To order, send $50 by check or money order to <u>Cardoza Publishing</u>

THE GRI ROULETTE MASTER
- Advanced Winning Roulette Strategy -

Here it is! **Finally**, Gambling Research Institute has released the **GRI Roulette Master** - a **powerful** strategy formerly used only by **professional** and high stakes players. This **strongman strategy** is **time-tested** in casinos and has proven **effective** in Monte Carlo, the Caribbean, London, Atlantic City, Nevada and other locations around the world. It's available here **now**!

EASY TO LEARN

The beauty of the GRI Roulette Master is that it's **easy to learn** and easy to play. Its simplicity allows you to **leisurely** make the **correct bets** at the table, while always knowing exactly the amount necessary to insure **maximum effectiveness** of our strategy!

BUILT-IN DYNAMICS

Our betting strategies use the **built-in dynamics** of roulette and ensure that only the best bets are working for us. There are no hunches or second guessing the wheel - all you do is follow the instructions, play the necessary bets, and when luck comes your way, **rake in the winnings**.

BUILT-IN SAFEGUARDS

The GRI Roulette Master's **built-in safeguards** protect your bankroll against a few bad spins while allowing you to **win steady sums of money**. Not only does this strategy **eliminate the pitfalls** of other strategies which call for dangerous and frightening bets at times, but also, allows you three styles of betting: **Conservative** for players seeking a small but steady low risk gain: **Aggressive** for players wanting to risk more to gain more: and **Very Aggressive** for players ready to go all out for **big winnings**!

BONUS!!! - Order now, and you'll receive the **Roulette Master-Money Management Formula** ($15 value) **absolutely free**! Culled from strategies used by the top pros, this formula is an **absolute must** for the serious player.

To order, send $25 by bank check or money order to <u>Cardoza Publishing</u>.